LOST RECIPES OF OUR ANCESTORS

A Collection of Recipes from Pioneers, Homesteaders and the Great Depression

NOTICE: You <u>Do NOT</u> Have the Right to Reprint or Resell this Report

COPYRIGHT© 2010-2021 JKW Enterprises, Inc. All Rights Reserved:

No part of this material may be reproduced or transmitted in any form whatsoever, electronic, or mechanical, including photocopying, recording, or by any informational storage or retrieval system without express written, dated, and signed permission from the author(s).

Disclaimer and/or Legal Notices:

While every attempt has been made to verify the information provided in this publication, neither the Author nor the Publisher assumes any responsibility for errors, omissions, or contrary interpretation of the subject matter herein. This publication is not intended for use as a source of legal or accounting advice. The Publisher wants to stress that the information contained herein may be subject to varying state and/or local laws or regulations. All users are advised to retain competent counsel to determine what state and/or local laws or regulations may apply to the user's particular business.

The Purchaser or Reader of this publication assumes responsibility for the use of these materials and information. Adherence to all applicable laws and regulations, federal, state, and local, governing professional licensing, business practices, advertising, and all other aspects of doing business in the United States or any other jurisdiction is the sole responsibility of the Purchaser or Reader. The Author and Publisher assume no responsibility or liability whatsoever on the behalf of any Purchaser or Reader of these materials. Any perceived slights of specific people or organizations are unintentional.

Introduction   **4**

How to cook without modern conveniences	6
Cooking without electricity	9
Cooking equipment for preppers	12
Survival Recipes of the pioneers	15
Survival Native American Recipes	25
Why Is Pemmican a Great Survival Food?	27
Great Depression Era Recipes	34
The Preppers Pantry: What food ingredients to stockpile for cooking in a crisis	47
Conclusion	55

INTRODUCTION

You may not have given this much thought, but an end-of-the-world event could take place any day. If you are not ready for that day, you're going to have a lot of trouble trying to survive. You may not have the comforts of a modern life anymore.

You need to be able to carry yourself without the need for modern tools. One of the most important components of survival is going to be food. You cannot live without food. Without modern equipment, it will be very hard for you to cook. You might not even have any access to electricity.

Luckily, we are here to educate you on how to survive without modern cooking equipment. This book will especially focus on teaching you a large collection of lost recipes from pioneers, farmers, Native Americans. These are simple yet delicious and hearty recipes you can make practically anywhere and do not require high-tech kitchen equipment or even electricity.

Your survival will greatly depend on your attitude. Your ability to withstand stress will dictate how long you can go without the comforts of modern life. You must have a positive mindset with clear goals of surviving. You can only achieve this clear mindset when you learn survival techniques. If you don't even know the basic survival techniques, you cannot possibly have a positive mindset.

This book will allow you to learn the most basic survival recipes. These recipes have been used by our ancestors to survive in the wild for a long time. They didn't have any modern equipment, yet they made such delicious survival foods. These traditional foods are enriched with essential nutrients and have a long history of keeping people healthy. You will need healthy food in emergency situations because your body needs to function properly to bear the hardships of survival. A positive mind is largely linked with a healthy diet.

This book will not just teach you traditional survival recipes but also teach you how to cook without electricity. You will learn to bake without a modern oven. How cool is that? You will also find a detailed list of essential kitchen equipment. So, when you find yourself in an emergency, you will already have all the important equipment you need.

By the time you are done reading this book, your arsenal of reliable and nutritious food recipes will have increased.

HOW TO COOK WITHOUT MODERN CONVENIENCES

You are not going to find any modern cooking tools in an end-of-the-world scenario. You will have to go back to the old ways to be able to cook your food. In this chapter, you'll learn about some of the most important forgotten techniques for cooking food.

How to bake without an oven

Bread is an important part of the diet all around the world. You should be aware of methods of baking bread that don't require a traditional oven. Keep in mind that baking bread is not a modern practice; it dates back centuries before electricity was even invented. You do not have to rely on a modern-day oven!

Grill: You may not have heard of this before, but baking on a grill is quite easy. It takes a little practice to perfect, but once you get the hang of it, it'll be super easy. Heat up your grill once you get your bread dough ready. It is nice to have a thermometer to keep checking the temperature of the dough. Make sure the flames below the grill are as low as possible to keep the bottom of the bread from burning. Generally, the bread takes about 30 minutes to bake. The main thing to remember is that the center temperature of the bread should be 200 degrees Fahrenheit in the end.

Skillet: If you are lucky enough to have still access to a stovetop or even the top of a wood stove, you can easily prepare bread in the skillet. Place your bread dough in a greased skillet. Let the bread dough rise. To avoid moisture from dripping on your bread, wrap a clean cloth around the lid that fits your skillet. Cook bread on low heat until your bread turns golden brown from the bottom. Then flip the bread and cook the other side of the bread until ready.

Sun oven: Sun oven will probably be your best option for making bread as it requires no fuel at all. You don't need any electricity or even firewood. All you need is a hot, sunny day. You can use any pan.
Sun ovens can also be found in markets; you might want to buy one for emergency situations. Get your oven ready before you put the bread dough in; it should ideally be at the same temperature that your recipe calls for in a normal oven. Place the sun oven in an open area; make sure it gets a consistent dose of sunlight. If you have a thermometer, you will be able to know when your bread is ready without any experience.

Earth oven: This type of oven can be built from all natural and even free materials. So, if you are stranded in a place with literally no baking equipment, an earth oven is the ideal choice for you. Moreover, they only require little fuel. Get small pieces of firewood for the oven. Let the fire burn away before you place the bread in. The earth oven absorbs the heat from the fire and bakes your bread. Also, sweep out any leftover ashes to avoid ruining your bread. If you are not sure if the oven is cool enough, toss in some cornmeal. It should turn brown without giving any smoke.

Dutch oven: This oven is best to cook over an open fire. It can also make bigger loaves of bread. Let the fire burn for a while, so you have a good bed of coals/firewood. Also, pile some coals on top of the oven to ensure it gets heated evenly. A good way to ensure even heat is to hang the Dutch oven over the fire using a tripod. Your bread should not take more than 15 to 30 minutes to bake.

Stick bread: Making stick bread is a quick and easy option if you are cooking over an open fire and lack modern equipment. You need to make your dough and twist it around a stick in a spiral. Hold it over your fire just as if you would do while toasting marshmallows.

Ash cakes: Over the years, travelers with no equipment but an open fire have cooked ash cakes to feed themselves. Basically, ash cakes can be cooked in three different ways. For the first method, press your dough into thin, pancake-type pieces and put them directly on burnt coal/firewood. For the second method, wrap your ash cakes in large, green leaves to avoid traces of ash on your bread. For the last method, you can take a flat piece of firewood and stick the dough to it. Place it next to the fire and allow it to cook slowly.

COOKING WITHOUT ELECTRICITY

There is a good chance that you won't find any electricity in an end-of-the-world event. You will need to be able to cook without electricity in order to survive. Luckily for you, we are here to educate you about a variety of methods to cook off-grid.

- **Wood biomass ovens and rocket stoves:** Biomass and wood are the most ancient ways of cooking food. At the very basic level, you can dig a shallow trench of fire under a Dutch oven to protect the fire from wind. The fire can be made from charcoal, wood, or even dung. For a reflector oven, you can use radiant heat from an open fire that is reflected towards your food.
- **Portable cooking bags:** One of the simplest methods of preparing food without electricity is to use food packaging with built-in heating elements. You can find products that require a twist, snap or shake to trigger a chemical reaction inside the package. These are exothermal reactions as they give out heat which warms up the food inside. Portable camping cooking bags are also a variation of such packaging products as they allow you to heat any food in a pouch heated by chemical reactions.
- **Wood burning stove:** Get a wood-burning stove as soon as you can. It is the most helpful tool you can find to cook food without power. It is just as effective as a gas or electric stove. You do not even have to go out of your house to cook. Just collect some good quality firewood, and you are good to go. Also, you can buy a

stove with an oven installed into it so you can also heat your food without electricity.

- **Portable butane stove:** It is just as big as a regular laptop; you can carry a portable butane stove just about anywhere. Even though it is very small in size, it can still properly cook your food. These are best for short emergencies as they cannot hold large amounts of fuel. You can store butane canisters in your house but be careful as they are inflammable. For safety precautions, you can buy a countersink release vent (CRV). It is a safety feature that allows gas to move through the small holes in the ca rim when the pressure/heat inside the canister gets too much.

- **Propane grill:** Most of you are already aware of propane grills. It requires little fuel to generate a surprisingly large amount of heat. However, do not use these grills indoors as it is not very safe and has an unpleasant smell. Keep your propane cylinders always outside and upright in a protected location. Avoid wet areas as it can catch rust easily, which will cause cylinder failure.

- **Alcohol stoves:** Alcohol stove is not only a great camping tool but can also be used for survival purposes. It is mostly used for heating things up, boiling water, making soup, and hot drinks like tea and coffee. This method is safer than other liquid fuels and is very inexpensive. Moreover, alcohol stove cooking is non-toxic, biodegradable, and water-soluble.

- **Charcoal stove:** Almost everyone knows about this classic backyard cooking option. It can come in very handy in crisis situations. A similar cooking method for charcoal is with a box oven. The unique thing about a box oven is that it can help bake cakes, bread, cookies, and pizza. You can make a basic cardboard oven all by yourself. Wrap foil on the inside of the box, cut it from the bottom completely. Put coals in the fire pit, let them burn until a smooth bed of coals is ready. Place your food on the oven's rack.
- **Solar oven:** If you find yourself stranded in a sunny area, you can use a solar oven for cooking food easily. It doesn't require any additional energy sources. It is made with aluminum reflectors to bake food. It can also be used to heat food and sterilize water. Aluminum reflectors concentrate the sunlight at one point. The sunlight gets converted into heat which gets trapped inside the food. Solar cooking has been around for centuries, but most people can't even imagine cooking in such a way.

COOKING EQUIPMENT FOR PREPPERS

It is very important to have backup tools in your kitchen. You need to consider what kind of emergency circumstances you can find yourself in and the limitations. For instance, if you reside in urban areas, you might want to have stoves that require gas fuels. If you live in suburban areas where there is a lot of nature around, you might want wood-fueled stoves. So, before going out or buy backup cooking equipment, consider the following factors:

- How many people do you need cooking equipment for? You should always try to pick lightweight equipment if you are a large group. Smaller groups of people do not require much equipment.
- What are the exact purposes? You need to evaluate if you will only be using this equipment for cooking or cleaning and other uses.
- What sort of fuel is best for you? Some of you might not prefer to keep inflammable gas cylinders in your house; people from urban areas might not prefer firewood as a source.
- Budget! The most important factor is to know what you can afford. You can find great options in a wide price range. Allocate your budget to the most important items if you do not have a big budget.

Lost Survival Recipes of Our Ancestors | Page 12

Since now you know what factors to consider when buying kitchen equipment, let's take a look at the basic kitchen equipment.

1. **Butchering kit:** Your butchering kit should have different types of knives, wood-bone saw, cutting board, etc.

2. **Matches:** Most people don't even use matches to light up their stoves, but this is how it was done until a few years ago. Book matches are the most economical matches.
3. **Hand grain mill:** It is used for grinding grains, coffee, herbs, spices, and even beans and legumes. It is a bit slow going, but the plus point is that it requires no electricity.
4. **Cast iron cookware:** Cast iron is very durable; it does not warp or disfigure and can last for decades. It can be placed directly over the fire.
5. **Canning equipment:** Arguably, the most important thing in survival situations is food preservation. Make sure you have a water bath canner, pressure canner, canning jars, and tattler reusable canning lids.
6. **Water filter:** You are going to need clean and sanitary drinking water. You can buy handy water filters from the market.
7. **Roasting pan:** Buy roasting pans made of stainless steel that will easily fit into your oven.
8. **Tea kettle:** Kettles made of stainless steel or copper work best. It not only makes instant tea, but the steam also warms and moisturizes the air.

9. **Hand utensils:** Avoid plastic hand utensils as they wear out easily and are not very healthy. You should have the following utensils with you all the time: ladles, serving forks, serving spoons, slotted spoons, spatulas, pastry cutter, sharpening steel, whisk, cheese slicer, rolling pin, potato peeler, and meat tenderizing hammer.
10. **Meat grinder:** You might have to process your own food. Buy the best quality meat grinders as you will have to grind raw meat.
11. **Nutcracker:** Find heavy-duty nutcrackers that can crack through the hardest of shells. A good nutcracker nets more food for your nut foraging efforts.
12. **Cloth napkins:** You are going to need cloth napkins that can efficiently soak up liquids. Find napkins that are made of 100% cotton.

SURVIVAL RECIPES OF THE PIONEERS

Prepping food in ancient times was nothing like how we do it today. Food preparation did not rely on modern cooking equipment. In this chapter, we will learn about some of the best survival recipes of pioneers.

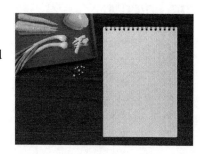

Potato cakes

Potatoes have always been an important crop in earlier times. They can be stored for longer times than most crops. Pioneers never traveled without potatoes. Potato cakes are similar to pancakes.

Ingredients:

- 6 peeled potatoes
- ½ cup milk
- 2 tbsp salt
- 2 eggs
- 1 cup of flour

How to make: First of all, wash and peel the potatoes before grating them. Mix salt, eggs, flour, and milk together. Pour the mixture into a hot pan with melted shortening. Cook the cakes until they turn golden brown on both sides.

Molasses stack cake

Pioneers used this food for special occasions like weddings. It was considered an expensive food item, so guests would bring their layers of cake and place them on top with slices of apple butter in between.

Ingredients:

- 1/2 cup buttermilk and shortening
- 1 egg, 1 cup molasses
- 2 cups flour
- 1/2 tsp baking powder
- Cinnamon
- Nutmeg

How to make: Heat your oven to 350 degrees Fahrenheit. Pour buttermilk, shortening mixture molasses, egg, and baking powder in one bowl and mix. Sprinkle some cinnamon and nutmeg on top. Then, put flour in the mixture and mix again. Cut out circles of the mixture and place them on the baking dish. Bake them until they turn golden brown.

Side pork and Mormon gravy

This is a very delicious and filling meal. Pioneers used to cook their bacon in special ways instead of just frying. This dish can be served with potatoes and cornbread.

Ingredients:

- Flour
- Milk
- 8 thick slices of side pork or bacon
- Fat drippings

How to make: Set aside fried slices of side pork or bacon in a pan. Keep them warm. Then pour four tablespoons of fat drippings into the pan. Add flour. After heating for a little while, add milk and stir for a few minutes. Put it back in low heat until the gravy is smooth and creamy.

Swiss apple cherry pie

Swiss were also among the pioneers who went on the Oregon trail. They had their own dessert recipes that were very well-liked among the pioneers; Swiss apple pie was one of them.

Ingredients:

- 4 large apples
- 6 Tbsp Butter
- 1 cup sugar
- 2 Tbsp. Flour
- 2 Tbsp. the ground cinnamon
- 1/2 tsp ground nutmeg
- Cherries
- Melted butter
- Evaporated milk

How to make: Slice large cooking apples into thin slices. Make double-crust pastry from the pie. Then brush the pastry shell with melted butter. Put apple slices on the pastry shell. Add sugar, nutmeg, flour, and ground cinnamon. Put a layer of fresh or canned cherries on top. Sprinkle all the dry ingredients. Finally, lay the top crust and brush with milk. Bake for 40 minutes at 425 degrees Fahrenheit.

Chuck wagon Beans

Originally, pioneers used to make chuck wagon beans on a campfire, but you can use a stove if available. It is a cattle recipe from the Midwest. You can eat these beans with rice or corn as the two foods mix up to give important proteins to your body.

Ingredients:

- 16-ounce dry pinto beans
- 9 cups water
- 2 large peeled onions
- 2 teaspoons salt
- ½ teaspoon oregano
- ½ teaspoon garlic powder or two cloves of sliced garlic
- ¼ teaspoon pepper
- 1 tablespoon brown sugar or molasses

How to make: Wash the dry pinto beans. Boil the beans in 6 cups of water. After boiling, turn off the stove and let the beans cool out for an hour. Then, pour three more cups of water and boil again. This is a very important step, do not skip it. After this, add the rest of the ingredients and mix thoroughly. Cook the mixture for about an hour.

Corn Dodgers

Corn dodgers are round bits of cornbread that can be served with stew or chili.

Ingredients:

- 2 cups cornmeal
- 2 tablespoon butter
- 1 tablespoon sugar
- ½ tsp salt
- 2 cups milk
- 1 tsp baking powder

How to make: Heat up your Dutch oven. Cook cornmeal, butter, sugar, salt, and milk together in a saucepan. Turn the heat off and let the mixture sit for at least five minutes. Then, add in baking powder. Cook again for about 15-20 minutes until all the edges turn brown.

Hasty pudding

It was a staple food among pioneers and is the predecessor of the pudding that we are used to today.

Ingredients:

- Water (3 cups worth)
- Salt (half teaspoon)
- Cornmeal (half cup)

How to make: Add half a teaspoon of salt to three cups of water and boil it over a medium to high flame. Keep stirring the spoon, so no clumps of salt remain behind. While boiling, steadily add a half cup of cornmeal. Stir for another twenty minutes until your pudding is ready. Turn the heat off and let the pudding cool down.

Soda biscuits

Biscuits are the perfect examples of any classic American breakfast. Pioneers used to prepare biscuits along with sausages, eggs, and gravy. You can prepare an entire batch of these soda biscuits in less than half an hour.

Ingredients:

- 3 1/3 cups flour
- 1 tsp salt
- 1 tsp baking soda
- Milk

How to make: Heat the oven to 430 degrees Fahrenheit. Fill a large bowl with flour and milk to make a stiff dough mixture. In a separate bowl, dissolve baking soda in milk. Then pour it into the dough mixture. Roll out dough until it turns into a layer. Cut circles and bake them in the preheated oven for 15 minutes.

Cornmeal Mush

It has a very simple recipe but needs to be made well, and the quality of cornmeal matters a lot. Pioneers always used to carry cornmeal around as it was long-lasting. Cornmeal can be served with cowboy stew, fish, or BBQ meat. It can also be dressed up with some sweet topping like apple and cinnamon for dessert.

Ingredients:

- 4 cups of boiling water,
- 1 cup of cornmeal,
- 1 tbsp of lard,
- 1 tsp of salt,
- Dried currants

How to make: Pour dried currants in boiling water and let cook for a few minutes. Then, put in cornmeal and stir continuously to keep it from clumping. Finally, mix in appropriate amounts of lard and salt and stir for about three minutes. If you want, you can also add butter and molasses for flavor. This is an optional step. Remove the mixture from heat and serve immediately.

Cured Bacon

Pioneers always used to carry hundreds of pounds worth of bacon in their wagons when traveling out west. It was an essential food. To prevent the meat from going bad under the sun, pioneers would first cure it and then pack it in a barrel to avoid the fat from melting.

Ingredients:

- Salt
- Saltpeter
- Molasses
- Brown sugar
- Ham

How to make: The saltpeter, molasses, and sugar go together in a bowl to form brine. Then sprinkle some salt on the ham. Take the brine mixture and pour it into the ham before putting it into the barrel to cure. It will take at least four weeks to cure completely. After it is properly cured, cut the ham into small strips and cook.

Mormon Johnnycake

Mormon Johnnycake is a variation of the standard pancake. What makes it different from the standard pancake is that it is made with cornmeal for a fluffy, filling addition to a stew or soup.

Ingredients:

- 2 cups of cornmeal
- ½ cup of flour
- 1 tsp of baking soda
- 1 tsp of salt
- 2 cups of buttermilk
- 2 tablespoons of molasses
- 2 eggs (optional)

How to make: First, mix all the dry ingredients and then pour in milk and molasses. You can also add eggs to make the Johnnycake a bit fluffier; it is up to you. Put batter in a greased 9" pan and cook in high heat for at least 20 minutes.

Lacey-Edged Corn Pancakes

Corn and corn products were the pioneer's staple food. Pioneers used to make lacy-edged corn pancakes from cornmeal.

Ingredients:

- 1 cup of white cornmeal
- 1/2 tsp of baking soda
- 1 egg, 1 1/4 cup of buttermilk
- 1/2 tsp of salt
- 1 Tbsp of bacon fat or lard

How to make: Put white cornmeal, baking soda, and salt together in a small bowl. Add in egg and buttermilk to make the batter. Using a hot cast-iron skillet, melt the lard or bacon fat and set it aside. Allow the shortening to smoke before adding batter in the melted lard or bacon fat. Place each spoonful of batter at a distance of 6 inches from each other to cook evenly.

Fart and Dart Beans

This recipe does not originally belong to the pioneers, but it takes inspiration from the original recipe. As you know by now, beans were a significant food item for pioneers. They had a large shell life and were a great source of protein.

Ingredients:

- 1 large bowl of canned Lima,
- Red kidney,
- White northern,
- Lima and butter beans,
- Pork and beans,
- 1 lb. bacon,

- Chopped large onions,
- Chopped garlic,
- Chopped 1 cup brown sugar
- 1/2 cup vinegar
- 1/2 tsp mustard

How to make: Add equal quantities of red kidney, canned lima, butter beans, white northern, and lima in a bowl and mix well. Then put in pork and beans to make 16 ounces of bean mixture. Fry the chopped bacon in a separate pan until it is cooked. Pour the original bean mixture into the pan with bacon and chopped garlic and onions. Stir brown sugar, mustard, and vinegar in another pan. Heat the pan for at least 15 minutes. Pour the obtained liquid into the bean mixture and bake it for 60 minutes.

Butter less, Eggless, Milk less Cake

In the days of the pioneers, eggs were not easily available. Pioneers used to make cakes without any milk, egg, or butter due to the lack of availability of these ingredients. This recipe is still enjoyed as a classic in many parts of America today.

Ingredients:

- 1 cup of brown sugar
- 1 cup of cold water
- 1/4 tsp of nutmeg
- 1 ½ of cup raisins
- 1 tsp of salt
- 1/3 cup of shortening
- 1 tsp of cloves
- 1 tsp of cinnamon
- 25 ml hot or lukewarm water
- 1 tsp of baking soda
- 2 cups of flour
- 1/2 tsp of baking powder

How to make: Add brown sugar to a cup of cold water with all the prepared raisins and boil it. Put in salt, cloves, nutmeg, shortening, and cinnamon after boiling. Boil this mixture for three more minutes and let it cool. Now, pour in the baking soda, flour, and baking powder. Bake the final mixture for at least 40 minutes at 350 degrees Fahrenheit.

Spotted Pup

If you do not want to let your leftover rice go to waste, this recipe is for you. You can turn your leftover rice into a sweet, sticky dessert. Pioneers were very careful about not wasting any food. Rather than eating cold leftover rice, pioneers used them in an entirely new, tasty recipe.

Ingredients:

- Cooked rice
- Milk nutmeg
- Raisins
- Vanilla
- Salt eggs
- Sugar

How to make: Put the cooked rice in a Dutch oven. Add milk enough to submerge all the rice grains. Then, pour in a beaten egg, vanilla, salt, nutmeg, and sugar, then top off with raisins. Place a lid over the Dutch oven and let the mixture heat until the egg is completely fried.

Mud apples

This recipe is exactly what it sounds like, apples covered in mud. As pioneers had very limited resources when they were crossing the stretch of the Oregon trail, they made most of what they had. Mud apples are not the most delicious, but desperate times call for desperate measures!

Ingredients:

- Apples
- Mud

How to make: First, cover all the apples thoroughly in mud. Cook these over a bonfire for at least 45 minutes. Scrape away any ash from the apples and peel the skin off the apples.

SURVIVAL NATIVE AMERICAN RECIPES

Before the arrival of white settlers on the shores of North America, the people who were already living there had been thriving for hundreds of years, using limited foodstuffs available to them. You might want to be aware of native American recipes as they are very easy to make, do not require any modern equipment, and taste great. These foods were very light, nutritious, and energy-dense.

Pemmican

The word 'Pemmican' is derived from the Cree Indian word 'Pimihkan.' It means greasy fat. In pemmican, the lean to fat ratio is 1:1. The ratio can be varied for some recipes. Pemmican has been the ultimate survival food for centuries. It was invented by the Native Americans. They would turn to pemmican when the regular food supply was scarce. It helped keep them warm and well-fed even in the worst of times. The fact that pemmican was very portable, had good preservative properties, had high calories, and had good taste made it very popular.

Surprisingly, pemmican has a very long shelf-life at room temperature. But still, you can store it in a fridge, freezer, root cellar, or basement. Native Americans used to wrap up their pemmican in canvas or hides.

Pemmican is basically fat and meat. Native Americans mostly made pemmican with buffalo fat or bear fat. Dried and powdered meat was used. The meat could be venison, buffalo, beef, or anything. It is fair to say that anything that had four legs was used by Native Americans for meat. The chosen meat was cut into strips, dried, pulverized into powdered form, and mixed with fat. Native Americans would also add wild berries and salt to add flavor and help preserve it. Honey and nuts can also be added for additional preservative properties. The whole meal simply becomes a nutritional wallop.

WHY IS PEMMICAN A GREAT SURVIVAL FOOD?

Pemmican is an excellent survival food for the following reasons:

- Very few ingredients – The simplest recipe involves only meat and fat.
- Rich in calories – When you are in a survival situation, sustainability is very important. Pemmican helps you sustain the required number of calories in your body. Pemmican has around 300 calories per serving.
- Easy to make – Pemmican is the world's oldest survival food. Back then, there were no electric appliances; it was cooked with the most basic tools. It only takes a little time and the right ingredients.
- Easy to carry – Pemmican can be easily packed in pockets or pouches of bags. It is super lightweight; even children can carry it.

How to cook?

Pemmican does take a little while to be cooked, but the recipe is actually pretty simple.

Ingredients:

2 pounds bacon and 1-pound suet or beef tallow (beef fat), which should give you about a cup of rendered fat, ¼ pound (4 ounces) of jerky, the remaining crispy, fried bacon from your rendering, 1 cup raisins, 1 cup craisins (dried cranberries), 1 cup peanuts, ¼ cup honey, 1 teaspoon Kosher salt

Directions:

1. Extract fat from the bacon and beef fat. Remove the bacon and drain it once it gets crisp.
   Put the jerky in fat and fry it until it gets crisp.
2. Take the fried jerky, put it on the plate with crisp bacon, and set the fat aside.
3. Take all the dry, crisp bacon and jerky and process in the food processor until all of it turns into bits.
4. Mix craisins, raisins, and nuts in a separate bowl.
5. Then, put the kosher salt and processed meat into the bowl.
6. Stir all the ingredients together thoroughly.
7. The rendered fat goes in the mix as well.
8. When mixing, make sure everything is incorporated and spread around the fat.
9. Pour ¼ cup of honey into the mix.

10. Again, mix everything together until all the honey is well-distributed.
11. Spread the mix in an aluminum foil pan until you have a smooth, uniform surface.
12. Freeze overnight to make the slicing and packaging easier.
13. Cut out snack-size bar shapes from the pemmican.
14. You can eat them right away or wrap them in wax paper and put them into a resealable plastic container until you are ready to eat.

Tips for eating pemmican

You can eat pemmican in the following three ways:

Rubaboo: Drip a chunk of pemmican about the size of your fist in boiling water. Add flour, onions, carrots, potatoes, and some salt for seasoning. You could also add a little chopped salt pork and sugar to give pemmican a soup-like consistency. It tastes great with sourdough bread.

Fried Pemmican Rechaud: Fry pemmican in its fat. For good flavor, add wild onions, potatoes, flour, and salt. It can be eaten like a sandwich.

Raw: This is how the Native Americans originally used to eat pemmican. A chunk of pemmican is held in one hand, and a piece is bitten off and chewed. As simple as that!

Jerky

Jerked meat is simply lean meat dried to the extent of slowing down deterioration. The word jerky comes from 'Charqui', a Spanish word that means flesh cut into flakes and dried without salt.

It is a big part of the legacy that the Native Americans left behind. Even though they were not the only people in the history of the world to dry meat, our fondness for jerky still traces its roots to the original American Indians. However, the locally available jerky isn't the same as what Native Americans used to eat. Modern jerky is enriched with preservatives, artificial flavors, and other chemicals to keep it soft and palatable.

Beef jerky is one of the best survival foods. It is portable, easy to eat, and can even be stored for extended periods of time. Moreover, the best thing about beef jerky is that it does not need any cooking or additional items to consume, and still, it is delicious. It is a rich source of protein and vitamin B12. It nourishes your body with essential energy to keep your body strong and resilient. Even after long periods of time, jerky retains its original levels of proteins and fats.

How jerky preserves meat?

The purpose of preserving jerky is to primarily protect it from harmful bacteria. Meat is much more vulnerable to attacks of harmful bacteria than regular vegetables and fruit as animals have many bacteria living inside their bodies. You do not want to eat bad meat, especially if you are in a survival condition, as it will harm your body greatly. You will become susceptible to bacterial diseases, and your energy will be drained. You do

NOT want that! You must make sure that all the bacteria are eliminated from your meat.

The number one way to preserve your jerky is to apply salt. Salt, along with a small dose of sugar, makes for a natural preservative. You don't have to use a bunch of chemicals with names you can't even pronounce. Basically, salt draws out water from the cells through the process of osmosis. The salt concentration is higher outside than inside the meat; water moves out of the meat across the cell membrane to balance the ionic level on each side of the membrane. Since water is also drawn out of bacterial cells, they die due to dehydration.

How to store jerky?

Commercially prepared and packaged jerky can be stored in its original packaging in a cool, dark place. Pantries and root cellars are good choices for storage. Just make sure that jerky is kept away from sunlight, stove, or any other heat sources. Exposure to heat will result in condensation inside the bag, which will ultimately make way for mold. If you ever notice any water droplets inside your jerky bag, immediately take it out and dry it. This will reduce the shelf life of your jerky a little bit but prevent the development of mold.

For homemade jerky, make sure that your jerky is good and dry. Use paper towels to dry it and then store it in vacuum packaging in the freezer. Freezer bags or other sealable bags will also work. As an extra measure, you could also store your jerky in a paper bag for some days before putting it in the freezer to help eliminate any moisture.

How to make jerky?

Cut lean meat into thin strips. Trim all the fat as it can turn rancid into storage. You can even soak the meat in brine to retard the deterioration even more. Native Americans didn't really have this option but if you do, avail it. It will greatly increase your jerky's shelf life. You can add many things in brine to add flavor and preservative properties. These additives include:

- Worcestershire sauce
- Brown sugar
- BBQ sauce
- Black pepper
- Cayenne pepper
- Liquid smoke
- Mustard seed
- Mustard powder
- Cinnamon
- Brown sugar
- Garlic powder
- Onion salt
- Chili powder
- Hot pepper sauce
- Vinegar
- Teriyaki sauce

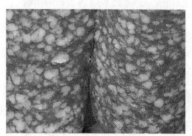

Moving on, make sure your meat is dried. It can be done in a dehydrator at a temperature of 165 degrees Fahrenheit. If you are not lucky enough to have a dehydrator, then you can even dry it in the sun, but it will take a bit longer.

Parched Corn/Rock hominy/Pinole

It is a well-known fact that corn/maize has been a staple food of native Americans for centuries. Even today, it is very popular all over North

America. The great thing about corn is that it can be made in several ways; you can boil it, grill it, stew it, steam it, cream it, grind it or even eat it raw. It is a very diverse food that can be useful to a prepper if they know what to do with it.

American Indian warriors and hunters regularly eat parched corn as extremely lightweight, high-energy trail food. To get an idea of what exactly parched corn is like, you can think of it as a partly popped kernel in popcorn, the ones with white stripes on them, except it is a lot tender and tastier.

How to make parched corn?

Basically, what you do is take dried corn kernels and roast them overheat, and eat them. But this is not it; you can do a variety of things with it. It can be seasoned with salt or any other flavor you like.

Here is a step-by-step procedure on how to prepare parched corn.

1. You need to dry your corn first. You can simply hang it in a dry area in your home or maybe dehydrate it in your oven. Once dried, store the corn on the cob.
2. Lightly rub the cob to separate all the kernels from the cob. If your corn is not dry enough, it will be harder to remove corn from the cob.
3. Fill a container full of cobs.

4. Set your oiled skillet over medium heat. Once the oil is hot enough, line the skillet entirely with oil and drain the excess oil. Add corn kernels barely enough to cover the bottom of the skillet.
5. Stir continuously for about 5 minutes. The corn will turn brownish and puff up.
6. Remove corn from the heat once it becomes brown properly, and then using paper towels, drain all the excess oil.
7. After draining all the oil, move corn to a different container. You can add brown sugar or any other flavorings you like. Put the lid on the container and shake it.
8. The final product is now ready to be consumed. It just takes a few minutes to make high energy delicious trail food that can fill you up for a long time.

GREAT DEPRESSION ERA RECIPES

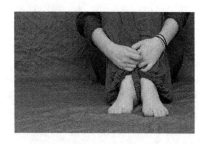

As you might've learned from the pandemic, life is indeed very unpredictable. You all should now understand that a future crisis could radically alter your life. You will have to go back to the old ways. The era of the Great Depression brought lots of misery. People in the Midwest and Southern Great Plains lost their farms and had to move to nearby towns where they could barely find any job. Food was scarce; people had to live off a limited supply.

It is not too unrealistic to say that you could face similar circumstances in the future or even worse. You should learn as much as you can from that time. In this chapter, we will particularly focus on the simplistic yet fulfilling and delicious recipes of the Great Depression era. Since people had limited sources and tools, their recipes were very simple and easy to make.

Here are some of the best recipes.

Potato Pancakes

Potatoes can be stored easily and are inexpensive, which makes them a staple food. People used leftover mashed potatoes to avoid any waste. You can do the same if you want to save as many resources as possible.

Ingredients:

- 2 cups of leftover mashed potatoes,
- 1 egg, ¼ cup of flour

- Salt and pepper to taste
- 2-3 Tablespoons of bacon grease or oil for frying

How to Make: Add all the ingredients in a bowl except for oil. Heat the grease in a skillet and carefully add the potato mixture to the hot oil. Then, add batter down with a spatula. Cook for a few minutes until both sides of the pancakes turn brown. Remove from heat and serve with syrup, applesauce, or any gravy.

Rice Pudding

You do not have to waste your leftover rice. Follow this recipe to make a delicious rice pudding out of leftover rice.

Ingredients:

- ¼ to ½ bowlful of cooked rice milk,
- A small dab of butter
- A bit of sugar or honey

Mix in all the dry ingredients. Pour milk until the mixture is the consistency you enjoy

Ham Hocks & Beans

It is a delicious and inexpensive meal. The beans don't even need to be presoaked when prepared this way. You can make this in just a couple of steps.

Ingredients:

- 1-pound of dry pinto beans
- 3-4 of ham hocks
- Chopped onion
- Pepper
- Salt

How to make: Rinse your beans thoroughly and remove any bad ones. Put the beans, ham hocks, pepper, and onion together in a large pot. Add water and boil. Make sure the heat is low so that the beans keep simmering. Allow the beans to simmer for some hours.

Your beans will be ready when they go tender, and the sauce around them thickens. Remove the ham hocks and get all the meat off the bones. Stir meat into beans.

Creamed Peas over Mashed Potatoes

This is a filling meatless meal that uses potato water instead of milk in the gravy. This water is not only nutritious but also has many other uses.

Ingredients:

- 2 TBS of butter
- 2 TBS of flour
- 2 cups of potato water (water you boiled potatoes in)
- Mashed potatoes 2 cups of peas – frozen, fresh, or canned, salt and pepper

How to make: Melt butter in a saucepan and then add flour until smooth, making a roux. Pour in potato water. Boil it as you stir constantly. Gradually, reduce the heat. Add in peas, salt, and pepper.

Serve along with hot mashed potatoes.

Simple Fish Chowder

During the depression, fishing was very common. The fish varied based on the location, but all of it would get eaten. Fish is indeed a very good survival food. According to this recipe, you can use your fish in simple chowder. It is very pantry friendly as it used evaporated milk instead of fresh milk.

Ingredients:

- 1 large onion chopped
- ½ of cup butter
- 6 cups of water
- 6 cups of potatoes
- Peeled and diced
- 2 pounds of fish
- Deboned and cut into chunks
- 3 TBS of lemon juice
- 2 cans of evaporated milk (12 ounces each)
- 2 tsp of salt
- 2 tsp of pepper

How to make:

Sauté the onion and melt butter. Put the melted butter and onion in a pot of water and boil it. Then, put in the potatoes and cook until it gets tender. Mix in fish and lemon juice. Cook on low heat for about 10 minutes. Finally, add evaporated milk, salt, and pepper. Heat through and serve.

Stretched Scrambled Eggs

This is a simple way to stretch eggs without losing its flavor.

Ingredients:

- 6 eggs beaten
- ¼ of cup flour
- 1/3 of cup water
- salt and pepper

How to make:

Mix flour and water until a smooth mixture is formed. Add eggs and mix thoroughly. Season with pepper and salt; finally, scramble the mixture as you would normally do. Your stretched scrambled eggs are now ready to be served with a slice of bread or fried potatoes.

Garbage Soup

Garbage soup helped minimize waste during the Great Depression. Each batch of garbage soup was unique, depending on what you consumed throughout the week. You might find yourself in a situation where the food supply is very low, and you have to make the most of the little food you have.

There's no true recipe per se. But here's a rough idea of how to make it.

Store all the vegetable scraps and bones in a container in your fridge. At the end of the week, put all the ingredients in a pot. Add lots of salt and pepper. Boil it in water, skin off all the foam, and let the soup simmer for some time. Take out all the bones before serving.

Foraged Salad

You might find yourself stranded in the wild where you won't have a good idea of what is edible around you. Take your time to note all the wilds around you that are edible and can be found in areas free of pesticides. Foraging your salad will give you a nutritious meal for free.

Ingredients can vary in this simple foraged salad based on what is available around you. Here's a simple recipe for the following wild edibles.

Ingredients:

- Dandelions (greens and yellow flowers)
- Shepherd's Purse
- Edible mushrooms
- Clovers lamb's quarter

How to make:

Clean all the wilds thoroughly and remove all the dead or browned leaves off them. Eat them as they are with a little vinegar and olive oil. You can add salt and pepper for taste.

Simple Homemade Bread

Bread is the staple food of many places all over the world. It was a cheap filler item found on the table for nearly every meal during the depression.

You can bake a large batch each week, so you'll always have bread available.

The following is a basic recipe requiring minimal ingredients. Add in 1 egg and ½ cup butter, if available, with water for extra flavor.

Ingredients:

- 16 2/3 of cup flour (5 pounds)
- 5 TBS of yeast
- 6 tsp of salt
- 5 cups of warm water

How to make:

Mix in 10 cups of flour, yeast, and salt. Pour in water and stir thoroughly. Gradually add flavor until the dough is thick. Knead the bread until it becomes smooth and is no longer sticky. Cover it with a lid and let it rise until it doubles in bulk which should take about an hour. Press down the dough and let it rest for at least ten minutes. Cut out loaves from the dough and place them into greased loaf pans. Let it rise for one hour. Finally, Bake at 350 degrees Fahrenheit for at least 30 minutes.

Goulash

Tomatoes can be grown and preserved easily. The following is an easy recipe from the Great Depression era. A side note: you can substitute other meat for the hamburger.

Ingredients: ½ pound of hamburger, 1 large onion, diced, 2 cups of uncooked macaroni, lots of fresh tomatoes, salt, and pepper

How to make:

In a pan, put brown hamburger and onion. Add tomatoes and allow the juice to run out in the pan. Juice should be enough to cover the macaroni.

Stir in macaroni and continue cooking on medium heat until the macaroni goes tender. For flavor, add salt and pepper.

Vinegar Pie

Since vinegar was easy to make at home, depression-era cooks often had lots of it. Only using a few basic ingredients you can make a delicious vinegar pie.

Ingredients:

- 2 TBS of butter
- ½ cup sugar
- 3 TBS flour
- 1 tsp cinnamon
- ½ tsp cloves
- 1 large egg
- 2 TBS vinegar
- 1 cup of water
- 1 unbaked pie crust

How to make:

Preheat your oven to 350 degrees Fahrenheit.

Mix flour, cinnamon, cloves, sugar, butter, egg, vinegar, and water in a saucepan and mix until you obtain a smooth mixture. Heat it in the oven and constantly stir until thick. Bake an unfilled pie crust for 5 minutes. Pour the thick filling into the crust and then bake further for 15 minutes. Your vinegar pie should be ready now.

Sugar Cream Pie

If you are lucky enough to have cream, follow the recipe to make a tasty sugar cream pie.

Ingredients:

- 2/4 of cup sugar
- 1/3 cup of flour
- 2 cups of cream
- Unbaked pie crust

How to make:

Preheat your oven to 350 degrees Fahrenheit. Add sugar and flour to a bowl and mix thoroughly. Gradually whisk in cream. When completely mixed, pour it into the pie crust.

Bake the filled pie for 50 minutes until the filling becomes firm.

Salted buttered tea, coffee, or hot cocoa

It is a strong, smoky tea with pink Himalayan salt and yak cream. It is a cheap source of good calories. Serving buttered coffee slows down the absorption of caffeine, so you do not get wired, and you have slow-burn energy.

Most claims about the benefits of buttered coffee are farfetched, but this is something different to try. It also has great taste! This tea can be made in the following ways

- 12 oz. of hot Coffee
- 2 Tbsp. unsalted butter
- 1 tsp sugar or molasses
- 1 tbsp. Heavy cream

Sour Crème Corn Bread

Ingredients:

- 12 cups of sour crème or plain yogurt
- 1-1/2 cups of cornmeal
- 1 tsp. of baking soda,
- 2 eggs
- 2 tablespoons of butter
- ¼ teaspoon salt

How to make:

Mix in all the dry ingredients first and then pour in well-beaten eggs and milk. Grease the cast iron pan with butter. Heat the pan and pour the mixture on it. Cook the mixture in the hot oven for at least 20 minutes.

Baking Powder Biscuits

Ingredients:

- 2 cups of cornmeal
- 4 tablespoons of butter
- 4 teaspoons of baking powder
- 1/2 teaspoon salt

- 2 cups flour
- 1 to ½ cups water or milk

How to make:

Mix in flour, cornmeal, salt, and baking powder. Use a kitchen knife to integrate cold butter into the mixture. Without wasting any time, mix with cold liquid (milk or water) to obtain soft dough. Line a wooden board with flour and roll the dough on it. Cut dough into round pieces. Bake until the dough turns into golden brown powder biscuits.

Vegetable Soup

Ingredients:

- 1 cup of tomato sauce or diced tomatoes with juice
- 1 quart of water
- ½ cup shredded cabbage
- 1 cup of potatoes
- ½ cup carrots
- Turnips or parsnips
- 1 medium-sized onion
- 4 tbsp. butter or oil
- ½ tsp of pepper
- A dash of kosher salt

How to make:

Add all the ingredients into boiling water right away. For the most flavorful results, sear the veggies first. Sautee the vegetables in butter or oil; after boiling, add salt and pepper. Your delicious vegetable soup is ready now.

Sweet Potato Soup

Ingredients:

- 1 large sweet potato (or 8 Oz. canned pumpkin or canned acorn squash)
- 1 cup of water
- ½ of cup milk
- A pat of Butter
- Dash of cinnamon
- Drizzle of maple syrup

How to make:

Cut out sweet potato slices and boil them in water. When potatoes get soft enough, mash them. Add in butter and maple syrup. You will need more maple syrup to get rid of the bitterness if you are using a pumpkin. Add sliced apples, too, if you want.

Beef Stew

Ingredients:

- ¾ to 1-pound meat from shin
- Knuckles neck, or cross ribs,
- ¾ cup of carrots
- 1 onion
- 1 cup of potatoes
- ½ cup of turnips
- ¼ tsp pepper
- 1 tsp of salt
- 1-quart water
- ½ cup flour

How to make:

Cut meat into small sections and soak half of the sections in water for about an hour. Boil it. Salt and pepper can be added now.

Coat the meat sections with flour and brown with onion in about 3 tablespoons of fat. Keep cooking for another 60 minutes. Add in vegetables meanwhile. Your beef stew should be ready after an hour.

THE PREPPERS PANTRY: WHAT FOOD INGREDIENTS TO STOCKPILE FOR COOKING IN A CRISIS

If you are planning to prepare for an end-of-the-world event, you must have a well-stocked kitchen. Here is a basic food checklist to help stock your pantry, refrigerator, and freezer for simple meals.

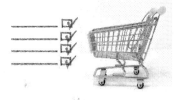

For pantry

1. Breakfast & Cereals

- Cereal
- Pancake mix
- Oatmeal

2. Canned, Jarred, & Pouched Foods

- Fruits and vegetables

- Meat, poultry, & seafood
- Dried fruit
- Nut butter (peanut, almond)
- Salsa
- Beans (pinto, black, garbanzo)
- Soups (look for lower-sodium varieties)
- Sauces (tomato, spaghetti, pizza)
- Broth or stock

3. Grains, Pasta & Sides

    - Bread (whole grain varieties)
    - Tortillas or taco shells
    - Oats
    - Pasta (whole grain varieties)
    - Rice

4. Produce

    - Onions
    - Potatoes

5. Snacks

    - Popcorn
    - Crackers (whole-grain varieties)
    - Nuts (almonds, walnuts, etc.)

6. Baking & Cooking Supplies

    - Oil for cooking
    - Seasonings & spices (salt, black pepper, garlic, minced onion)
    - Instant nonfat dry milk
    - Flour (whole grain)
    - Sugar (white granulated, brown)

- Vinegar

7. Condiments & Salad Dressings

- Ketchup
- Salad dressing
- Mayonnaise (low-fat option)
- Mustard

For Refrigerator

- Milk (fat-free or low-fat)
- Vegetables
- Butter or margarine
- Cheese (low-fat options)
- Eggs
- Fruits
- Yogurt (fat-free or low-fat)

For Freezer

- Meat & seafood
- Fruit
- Bread (whole grain varieties)
- Vegetables
- 100% fruit juice concentrate
- Waffles (whole-grain varieties)

You can personalize this list with the food most suitable for you.

Basic Ingredients substitutions

You cannot simply rely on the basic ingredients in a crisis. You might find yourself in situations where you do not even have these basic ingredients. It will be challenging to cook meals from basic staples when the recipe requires an item you do not have. Therefore, you should learn about the substitutes for the most common ingredients. It will help you a lot in surviving.

Cheese

As an alternative to commercially produced cheese, you can make cheese all by yourself from powdered milk. You should store canned cheese, bottled cheese spread, powdered cheese mixes, Velveeta, or freeze-dried cheese.

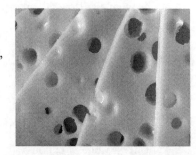

Cornstarch

Cornstarch plays the role of thickener in sauces.

For 1 tablespoon of cornstarch

- 2 tablespoons of all-purpose flour
- 2 teaspoons of arrowroot starch
- 1 tablespoon of potato starch
- 2 tablespoons of tapioca flour
- 3 tablespoons of rice flour

Cream (Sour)

For 1 cup of sour cream

- 1 cup of plain or Greek yogurt
- 1 cup of fresh cream
- 1 cup of buttermilk
- 1 cup of milk + 1 Tbs of vinegar
- 1 cup of whole milk + 1 tablespoon of lemon juice
- 1 cup of heavy whipping cream + 1 tablespoon of lemon juice
- 1 cup of cottage cheese + ¼ cup yogurt plus 1 teaspoon of lemon juice

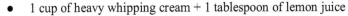

Cream (Half-and-Half)

For 1 cup of half-and-half cream

7/8 cup of whole milk + 2 tablespoons of melted unsalted butter

1 cup of evaporated milk

½ cup of whole milk and heavy cream

Cream (Heavy)

For 1 cup of heavy cream

- 2/3 cup of whole milk + 1/3 cup of melted unsalted butter
- 1 cup of whole milk and 1 tbs of melted butter

Eggs

Eggs play a big role in our kitchen; you can use them as leavening agents, as binders, to add moisture and to improve the taste of baked goods. Depending on how you want to use eggs, you can choose from the substitutions mentioned below.

For 1 egg

- 2 tablespoons of egg powder
- ¼ cup of pureed fruit + ½ teaspoon of baking powder
- 3 tablespoons of creamy nut butter
- 1 tablespoon of unflavored gelatin in boiling water
- ¼ cup of plain yogurt
- ¼ cup of buttermilk
- ¼ cup of carbonated water

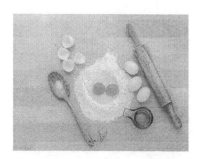

Alcohol

You may not like it, but you can use non-alcohol replacements for alcohol in your recipes.

- White wine = lemon juice mixed with water or chicken broth
- Red wine- grape or pomegranate juice
- Wine = apple juice or chicken broth
- Whiskey = prune juice
- Cognac = pear nectar or apricot
- Sake = rice or vinegar
- Kirsch- cherry juice
- Beer = club soda or seltzer

Butter

For 1 cup of butter

- 1 cup of unsweetened applesauce
- 1 cup of pumpkin purée
- 1 cup of mashed banana
- 1 cup of mashed avocado
- 1 cup of prune purée
- 1 cup of puréed white beans
- 1 cup of puréed pinto beans
- 1 cup of puréed black beans
- 1 cup of nut butter

Honey

For long-term food storage, honey is one of the best options.

For 1 cup of honey

- ¾ cup of light or dark corn syrup + ½ cup of granulated sugar
- 1 ¼ of cup sugar + 1/3 cup of liquid

Lard

For ½ of cup lard

- ½ cup of solid vegetable shortening
- 1 tablespoon of unsalted butter
- ½ cup of oil (coconut, olive, vegetable)

Whole milk

For 1 cup of whole milk

- 1 cup of evaporated milk + ½ cup of water
- 1 cup of reconstituted powdered milk + 1 teaspoon of honey + 2 teaspoons of vegetable oil
- 1 cup of skim milk + 2 tablespoons of melted butter
- 5/8 cup of skim milk + 3/8 cup of half-and-half
- 2/3 cup of 1% milk + 1/3 cup of half-and-half
- ¾ cup of 2% milk + ¼ cup of half-and-half
- 7/8 cup of skim milk and a little bit of heavy cream

Cooking oil

Cooking oils are used interchangeably without visibly affecting the overall texture of the finished product.

Cooking oil = margarine, shortening, or butter

Paprika

If you are like most people, you love paprika's taste in your food. Some of these substitutions may end up altering the taste of your food.

For 1 teaspoon of paprika

- 1/3 teaspoon of ground cayenne pepper
- 1 teaspoon of ground white or black pepper
- 1/3 teaspoon of red pepper flakes
- 1 teaspoon of chili powder
- 1 teaspoon of Cajun spice
- 1 teaspoon of Chipotle powder

- 1 teaspoon of hot sauce

Sugar

For 1 cup of dark brown sugar

- 1 cup of small-pieced sugar + 2 tablespoons of molasses
- 1 cup of light brown sugar
- For 1 cup of dark brown sugar
- 1 cup of small-pieced sugar + 2 tablespoons of molasses
- 1 cup of light brown sugar

CONCLUSION

If you have come this far, you are now one step closer to surviving in a crisis without the comforts of modern tools. Yep, be happy for yourselves.

Life is so unpredictable, as demonstrated by the arrival of Covid. You should be prepared for anything in life. Who knows what will happen tomorrow? A smart person is one who can make the most of his/her situation to survive. We have become so dependent on modern equipment that it is so hard to imagine life without them. But you must leave this mindset behind. You can do so much more. After all, people did live on Earth in older times when modern equipment wasn't available. Yet, they only survived but thrived. People in the Great Depression era, pioneers, and Native Americans are proof that we can survive in nature without electricity. Our ancestors have left us with food recipes that are very healthy and flavorful. Sadly, people have forgotten the old ways. The foods they used to consume are far more nutritious than the regular food you'll find today in markets. This is the main reason why we highlighted their examples in this book.

28% of Americans cannot cook, according to a 2011 survey. How sad is that? You will not find commercially cooked products in a survival situation. Julia Child, an American cookery expert, once said, 'Non-cooks think it's silly to invest two hours' work in two minutes' enjoyment; but if cooking is evanescent, so is ballet.'

You must learn how to cook food on your own. The recipes we talked about above are super easy and delicious. It does not require long and hard procedures. Understandably, beginners find cooking particularly hard, but that is how everyone feels trying new and unfamiliar things. So, do not be scared. Go to your kitchen and just take the first step. Put any recipe in front of you and get cooking. And keep doing it! Experience will make you a master cook in little time.

If you, however, already know how to cook, that is awesome. You do not need to spend time learning the basics. You can get right to learning our survival recipes. These survival recipes are very authentic. Also, try to cook these recipes without your electrical appliances. Use the cooking techniques mentioned at the start. This will help you master the true art of cooking. You will be able to cook anywhere, anytime. To be able to cook without electricity is going to be one of the most crucial survival techniques. In most end-of-the-world situations, you won't find any electricity. So, you should get right on learning to cook without electricity.

It is also important to remember that your regular ingredients might not be enough to survive a crisis. You will have to have substitutions that have a long shelf life. There will be times when you find yourself with excess food which you can't allow to go to waste. Therefore, you must be aware of good preservation techniques or simply choose foods that stay edible for longer periods of time. From the above-mentioned list of substitution ingredients, choose the most appropriate one's for you.